Tipsy Bartender
I'M HAVING *a* GIRL OVER

Sometimes a six-pack of cheap beer just won't do. Impress her with these easy to make cocktails.

Written & Photographed by Skyy John

Copyright © 2014 Tipsy Bartender Inc.
All rights reserved.

ISBN: 1492751707
ISBN 13: 9781492751700
Library of Congress Control Number: 2013918895
CreateSpace Independent Publishing Platform
North Charleston, South Carolina

This book is dedicated to all the fans of the *Tipsy Bartender* show. Your love, support, and advice have made us the Internet's number one bartending show. Thank you. We love you guys!

Table of Contents

Introduction	v
Bar Tools	1
Ingredients	2
Martinis	3
Mojitos	19
Margaritas	22
Frozen Drinks and Ice Cream	27
Cocktails	32
Shots	46
Bombs	59
Special Note to the Reader	62
Index	63

Introduction

Tell a guy that you are having a party and his response will invariably be something like this, "You invited chicks, right?" "You got any girls coming?" "What's the female situation?" "Will it be a sausage fest?" As a guy, I can tell you that we think about women almost every waking moment of everyday. Then we sleep and dream about them. With so much of our focus devoted to the opposite sex, why is it that we never consider their cocktail preferences? We assume, "Since the boys love strong whiskey cocktails, she must love them too." "Since the boys love cheap beer, then she must love it too." The purpose of this book is to right those incorrect assumptions and give guys a list of cocktails and shots that will entertain and excite the ladies. They'll want to be at your next party just for the drinks.

This book is not a collection of foo-foo drinks that no guy wants to be caught dead with in his hands. It is a book of drinks where the strong taste of alcohol is properly masked, creating super-smooth cocktails that taste great. This book is for the guy that has a girl coming over who doesn't really drink and he wants to make her something special. This book is for the new drinker who is still acquiring a taste for alcohol. This book is for all the people out there who want an alcoholic drink but do not wish to have that strong alcohol taste that burns your throat and chest. If you've ever heard someone say, "I don't like the taste of alcohol," make him or her a drink from this book; they'll love it.

The recipes in this book are very simple and easy to make. Also, the ingredients are cheap and available everywhere. I hate opening cocktail books and seeing ingredients that are ultra-expensive or next to impossible to find. Some books send you off in search of some exotic plant that you must then turn into syrup in order to make the drink. I want a cocktail. I don't want to have to go on a safari hunt first! Thankfully, this book is nothing like that; it caters to everyone. The guys in Australia, Canada, South America, Africa, Europe, Asia, the Caribbean, wherever you are, can find these ingredients and make these drinks just as easily as the guys here in Los Angeles or in New York.

Bar Tools

If you don't have any of the items in the picture, don't sweat it. There are ways to cheat.

A) Cocktail Shaker: The shaker is a very important part of your home bar. It allows you to mix, chill, and strain drinks. If you don't have a shaker, then simply pour your drink back and forth between two glasses to properly mix and chill it. You can then strain it by using a butter knife to keep the ice in as you pour the drink into your serving glass. It's not ideal, but it works.

B) Muddler: This stick-like tool is used to mash fruits or leaves in your glass or shaker. When muddling, be sure not to grind anything to a pulp, especially leaves. Just muddle enough to get some of the oil or juices out to add flavor to your drink. If you don't have a muddler, use the back of a spoon. Again, it's not perfect, but it works.

C) Glassware: I used a lot of different glass types in this book. I can honestly tell you that none of them will make your drink taste any better. The glasses in your cupboard will do just fine!

Ingredients

SIMPLE SYRUP

Simple syrup is used throughout this book as a sweetner. It's easy to make. I use the ratio 2:1, which means *2* parts sugar and *1* part water. Bring one cup of water to a boil, then add two cups of sugar. Stir until the sugar has dissolved; now you have simple syrup. If you were to try to sweeten a drink using just sugar, it never dissolves properly. Simple syrup on the other hand blends perfectly into any drink.

Note* You can adjust the sweetness of any of these recipes by using less or more simple syrup, depending on your preference. You can also replace simple syrup with agave in most of the recipes.

SOUR MIX:

Sour mix is also know as "Sweet & Sour." It's equal parts simple syrup and lemon juice. Just add some lemon juice to your simple syrup and now you have sour mix.

FLAVORED VODKA:

I used flavored vodkas in a few of the recipes. If all you have is regular vodka, don't let that deter you; still make the drink. It won't be perfect, but it'll still be a great cocktail.

Martinis

The purist will tell you that the martini is made with gin and any deviation from this is not really a martini. Who cares? That guy has no idea how to have fun. Don't invite him to your party. We're gonna break the rules. For the purpose of this book, if it's in a martini glass, it's a martini!

Note* If a martini is too weak, add more booze. If it is too strong, add more of the mixer. Modify it to your exact liking.

*Any of these martini recipes can be made into a regular cocktail. In most cases, all you need to do is build it in a cocktail glass over ice.

WATERMELON MARTINI

- 1½ oz. (45 ml) Vodka
- ½ oz. (15 ml) Simple Syrup
- 1 cup Watermelon

Muddle watermelon until it is a liquid. Shake all the ingredients with ice. Pour everything except the ice into a glass. Garnish with watermelon slice.

It's just three simple ingredients, but it has this exotic flair about it and is just plain delicious.

Tipsy Bartender: "I'm Having a Girl Over"

CAKE BATTER MARTINI

- ½ oz. (15 ml) Cake Vodka
- ½ oz. (15 ml) White Crème de Cacao
- ½ oz. (15 ml) Amaretto
- ½ oz. (15 ml) White Chocolate Liqueur
- 3 oz. (90 ml) Heavy Whipping Cream

Shake the ingredients with ice and strain into a glass rimmed with sprinkles. Use corn syrup to hold sprinkles in place.

The ladies love this drink. It tastes great, but it's really the sprinkles that sell it. Without the sprinkles, all you have is a glass of what looks like milk. Everyone's asking, "Who is this guy drinking milk at a party?" Now put some sprinkles on that glass, and you have a work of art and everybody wants one.

RASPBERRY MARTINI

- 5 Raspberries
- ½ oz. (15 ml) Simple Syrup
- 1½ oz. (45 ml) Vodka
- 3 oz. (90 ml) Lemon-Lime Soda
- Splash of Orange Juice

Muddle raspberries. Stir all the ingredients with ice. Pour everything except the ice into a glass. Garnish with raspberries.

Martinis

TIPSY BREAKFAST MARTINI

- 1 tsp. Orange Marmalade
- 1 oz. (30 ml) Gin
- ½ oz. (15 ml) Triple Sec
- 3½ oz. (105 ml) Orange Juice

Shake the ingredients with ice and strain into a glass. Garnish with toast buttered with marmalade.

After an intense night out, this is the perfect breakfast cocktail. Some jam, some bread, and some booze to keep the party going at the breakfast table.

GERMAN CHOCOLATE CAKE MARTINI

- 1 oz. (30 ml) Cake Vodka
- ½ oz. (15 ml) Amaretto
- 2½ oz. (75 ml) Milk
- 1 tbsp. Cream of Coconut
- 2 tbsp. Chocolate Syrup
- 1 tbsp. Caramel Syrup

Shake the ingredients with ice and strain into a glass rimmed with coconut flakes and garnished inside with caramel and chocolate syrup.

The German chocolate is not actually from Germany. An American named Sam German created it in 1852. Years later his recipe had a rebirth; meaning it was stolen and marketed as if it had German origins. Some bartender then stole the name and slapped it on this drink.

Tipsy Bartender: "I'm Having a Girl Over"

COCONUT MARTINI

- ½ oz. (15 ml) Vanilla Vodka
- 1 oz. (30 ml) Coconut Rum
- ½ oz. (15 ml) Cream of Coconut
- 3 oz. (90 ml) Pineapple Juice

Shake the ingredients with ice and strain into a glass rimmed with coconut flakes. Add cherry.

I stumbled on this drink at a bar in Maui. The bartender was so wasted he couldn't tell me the ingredients or even his name. I went home and came up with this version of his drink.

TROPICAL JADE MARTINI

- ½ oz. (15 ml) Vanilla Vodka
- ½ oz. (15 ml) Coconut Rum
- ½ oz. (15 ml) Midori
- ½ oz. (15 ml) Simple Syrup
- ½ oz. (15 ml) Lemon Juice
- 2½ oz. (75 ml) Pineapple Juice

Shake the ingredients with ice and strain into a glass rimmed with sugar. Add cherry. The Jade Martini is a classic drink, ideal for the ladies. I wanted to put my twist on it, so I made some modifications and came up with the Tropical Jade Martini.

Martinis

APPLETINI

- 1 oz. (30 ml) Vodka
- ½ oz. (15 ml) Sour Apple Pucker
- 3½ oz. (105 ml) Apple Juice

Shake the ingredients with ice and strain into a glass. Add green apple slice.

Usually this very popular ladies drink is made with sour mix, as most bars in America don't have apple juice as one of their mixers. However, I feel apple juice is what makes this drink work.

CRAN-APPLETINI

- ½ oz. (15 ml) Vodka
- ½ oz. (15 ml) Apple Pucker
- ½ oz. (15 ml) Peach Schnapps
- 3½ oz. (105 ml) Cranberry Juice

Shake the ingredients with ice and strain into a glass. Add red apple slice.

Tipsy Bartender: "I'm Having a Girl Over"

CARAMEL APPLETINI

- ½ oz. (15 ml) Vodka
- ½ oz. (15 ml) Butterscotch Schnapps
- ½ oz. (15 ml) Sour Apple Schnapps
- 3½ (105 ml) Apple Juice

Shake the ingredients with ice and strain into a glass garnished inside with caramel syrup. Add green apple slice.

This drink is often made using just vodka, butterscotch schnapps, and sour apple schnapps. That's not a perfect mix. Apple juice is needed to even everything out.

ICE CREAM MARTINI

- 3 Scoops of your favorite ice cream
- 1½ oz. (45 ml) Vodka (any flavor you like)

Put ice cream scoops in a glass. Pour vodka over ice cream. As the ice cream melts, sip the drink.

This is a drunken creation. I was drinking and suddenly had the craving for ice cream, but I wanted it mixed with my booze; thus, the ice cream martini was born. This is definitely a fun cocktail.

Martinis

TIRAMISU MARTINI

- ½ oz. (15 ml) Vanilla Vodka
- ½ oz. (15 ml) Crème de Cacao
- ½ oz. (15 ml) Coffee Liqueur
- Splash of Almond Liqueur
- 3½ oz. (105 ml) Cream

Shake the ingredients with ice and strain into a glass rimmed with cocoa powder and sugar. Top with whipped cream.

CHOCOLATE MARTINI

- ½ oz. (15 ml) Vanilla Vodka
- ½ oz. (15 ml) Irish Cream
- ½ oz. (15 ml) Crème de Cacao
- 1 tbsp. Chocolate Syrup
- 3½ oz. (105 ml) Milk

Shake the ingredients with ice and strain into a glass rimmed with sugar and garnished inside with chocolate syrup.

Tipsy Bartender: "I'm Having a Girl Over"

WHITE CHOCOLATE MARTINI

- ½ oz. (15 ml) Vanilla Vodka
- 1 oz. (30 ml) White Chocolate Liqueur
- 3½ oz. (105 ml) Cream

Shake the ingredients with ice and strain into a glass. Top with whipped cream and chocolate shavings.

WHISKEY MARTINI

- ½ oz. (15 ml) Whiskey
- 1 oz. (30 ml) Amaretto
- 2 oz. (60 ml) Pineapple juice
- 1½ oz. (45 ml) Lemon-Lime Soda
- Splash of Grenadine

Stir all the ingredients except the grenadine with ice and strain into a glass. Add splash of grenadine and cherry.

Typically when you think of the ladies, you don't think whiskey, but this drink is smooth and works perfectly. I had to include whiskey somewhere!

Martinis

ORANGE CREAMSICLE MARTINI

- 1 oz. (30 ml) Vanilla Vodka
- ½ oz. (15 ml) Triple Sec
- 1 oz. (30 ml) Cream
- 1 oz. (30 ml) Orange Juice
- 1½ oz. (45 ml) Whipped Cream

Shake the ingredients including the whipped cream with ice and strain into a glass. Top with whipped cream.

LEMON MERINGUE PIE MARTINI

- ½ oz. (15 ml) Vanilla Vodka
- 1 oz. (30 ml) Limoncello
- ½ oz. (15 ml) Simple Syrup
- 3 oz. (90 ml) Cream

Shake the ingredients with ice and strain into a glass rimmed with graham crackers. Top with whipped cream and graham crackers.

Tipsy Bartender: "I'm Having a Girl Over"

GLAMOUR GIRL MARTINI

- 4 oz. (120 ml) Pinot Grigio
- ½ oz. (30 ml) Peach Schnapps
- Splash of Cranberry Juice

Build ingredients in glass. Add cherry.

This is another really simple drink, but it looks and feels super classy. There is nothing more stunning than seeing a beautiful woman in an elegant dress holding a sexy martini like this one. I honestly believe something about the contours of the martini glass make a woman more appealing.

COTTON CANDY MARTINI

- 1½ oz. (45 ml) Vodka
- 1 oz. (30 ml) Pineapple Juice
- 2½ oz. (75 ml) Cranberry Juice

Shake the ingredients with ice and strain into a glass. Serve with a side of cotton candy.

Know that as soon as the cotton candy makes contact with liquid, it begins to melt.

Martinis

KEY LIME PIE

- 1 oz. (30 ml) Vanilla Vodka
- ¾ oz. (22 ml) Key Lime Liquor
- 2 oz. (60 ml) Pineapple Juice
- 1 oz. (30 ml) Heavy Whipping Cream

Shake the ingredients with ice and strain into a glass rimmed with graham crackers. Add lime slice.

MEXI-TINI

- ½ oz. (15 ml) Orange Vodka
- 1 oz. (30 ml) Tequila
- 3½ oz. (105 ml) Orange Juice

Shake the ingredients with ice and strain into a glass. Add lime slices.

Tequila comes from blue agave. Many people complain that tequila gives them nasty headaches. That cheap gold tequila you've been drinking all night is a *mixto*. It's only 51% blue agave, and the other 49% is junk. If you want to avoid that nasty headache, try a tequila that is 100% blue agave, such as a Silver tequila, a Reposado, or an Añejo.

Tipsy Bartender: "I'm Having a Girl Over"

LEMON DROP MARTINI

- 1 oz. (30 ml) Vodka
- ½ oz. (15 ml) Triple Sec
- 1 oz. (30 ml) Simple Syrup
- 2½ oz. (75 ml) Sour Mix

Shake the ingredients with ice and strain into a sugar-rimmed glass. Add lemon slices.

SNICKERDOODLE

- 1 oz. (30 ml) Irish Cream
- ½ oz. (15 ml) Butterscotch Schnapps
- ½ oz. (15 ml) Amaretto
- 2½ oz. (75 ml) Cream

Shake the ingredients with ice and strain into a glass rimmed with sugar and cinnamon. Add cinnamon stick.

When we think of snickerdoodles, cookies are what come to mind. This drink gets its name from the cookies and is just as tasty as its namesake.

Martinis

BRANDY ALEXANDER

- 1 oz. (30 ml) Brandy
- ½ oz. (15 ml) Crème de Cacao
- 3½ oz. (105 ml) Cream

Shake the ingredients with ice and strain into a glass. Sprinkle nutmeg on top.

This drink is most popular during the winter. People love brandy when it's cold for some reason.

One question you sometimes get asked as a bartender is, "What is a cognac?" A cognac is a brandy. However, only brandies produced in the Cognac region of France are allowed to bear the name cognac.

KIWI-TINI

- ½ Kiwi
- ½ oz. (15 ml) Simple Syrup
- ½ oz. (15 ml) Vodka
- 1 oz. (30 ml) Southern Comfort
- 2 oz. (60 ml) Pineapple Juice

Muddle kiwi. Shake the ingredients with ice and strain everything except the ice into a glass. Garnish with kiwi slice.

Tipsy Bartender: "I'm Having a Girl Over"

COSMOPOLITAN

- 1 oz. (30 ml) Lemon Vodka
- ½ oz. (15 ml) Triple Sec
- ½ oz. (15 ml) Lime Juice
- 3 oz. (90 ml) Cranberry Juice

Shake the ingredients with ice and strain into a glass. Add lemon slice.

This is a classic cocktail that was made popular by the TV show *Sex and the City*. This girl I was dating asked me to one of the *SATC* movies. I've never seen so many women in one place. You want to meet girls? Go to chick flicks.

PEARTINI

- 1½ oz. (45 ml) Vodka
- 2 oz. (60 ml) Canned Pear Syrup
- ½ oz. (15 ml) Simple Syrup
- 1 oz. (30 ml) Lemon Juice

Shake the ingredients with ice and strain into a glass. Add pear half.

Martinis

LYCHEE MARTINI

- 1 oz. (30 ml) Vodka
- ½ oz. (15 ml) Peach Schnapps
- 2½ oz. (75 ml) White Cranberry Juice
- 1 oz. (30 ml) Lychee syrup from the can

Shake the ingredients with ice and strain into a glass. Add two canned lychees.

If you can't find white cranberry juice, use regular cranberry juice. There will only be a slight difference in taste. White cranberries are slightly less tart than red cranberries.

TEQUILA SOUR APPLE MARTINI

- ½ oz. (15 ml) Tequila
- ½ oz. (15 ml) Triple Sec
- ½ oz. (15 ml) Sour Apple Pucker
- ½ oz. (15 ml) Lime Juice
- 3 oz. (90 ml) Apple Juice

Shake the ingredients with ice and strain into a glass. Add green apple and lime slices.

Tipsy Bartender: "I'm Having a Girl Over"

FRENCH MARTINI

- 1 oz. (30 ml) Vodka
- ½ oz. (15 ml) Raspberry Liqueur
- 3½ oz. (105 ml) Pineapple Juice

Shake the ingredients with ice and strain into a glass. Garnish with raspberries.

BELLINI MARTINI

- ½ oz. (15 ml) Vodka
- 1 oz. (30 ml) Peach Schnapps
- 3½ oz. (105 ml) Peach Nectar

Shake the ingredients with ice and strain into a glass rimmed with sugar. Add peach slice.

When people think of Cuba, they think of Castro and cigars. But it is also the birthplace of one of greatest cocktails ever: the mojito. It was also a favorite drink of author Ernest Hemingway, who once wrote on the wall of the bar La Bodeguita del Medio, "My mojito in La Bodeguita, My daiquiri in El Floridita." Do you realize how epic that was? He walked into the bar like a boss and put his graffiti on the wall in front of everyone, not hidden in the bathroom like I do with mine.

Note * Remember, you can adjust the sweetness of this drink by increasing and lessening the amount of simple syrup you use. Also, when muddling, don't grind the leaves and limes to a pulp. Just muddle enough to get some of the oils and juices out.

Tipsy Bartender: "I'm Having a Girl Over"

MOJITO

- 10 Mint Leaves
- 2 Lime Wedges
- 1½ oz. (45 ml) Simple Syrup
- 1½ oz. (45 ml) White Rum
- 2½ oz. (75 ml) Soda Water

Muddle limes, mint leaves, and simple syrup in a glass. Add ice and other ingredients. Garnish with lime slices and a mint sprig.

The first time I had a mojito was at a salsa dance bar in Guatemala. I don't salsa dance; I just went to watch. After my fifth mojito, I was the best salsa dancer ever. I had to take my shirt off because it was stifling my dance moves. I still don't know how I got back to the hotel that night.

MANGO MOJITO

- 4 oz. (120 ml) Mango
- 10 Mint Leaves
- 2 Lime Wedges
- 1½ oz. (45 ml) Simple Syrup
- 1½ oz. (45 ml) White Rum
- 2½ oz. (75 ml) Soda Water

Muddle the mango, limes, mint leaves, and simple syrup in a glass. Add ice and other ingredients. Garnish with mint sprigs, lime slices, and mango.

Mojitos

LYCHEE MOJITO

- 3 Lychees
- 2 Lime Wedges
- 10 Mint Leaves
- 1½ oz. (45 ml) Simple Syrup
- 1 oz. (30 ml) White Rum
- ½ oz. (15 ml) Lychee Liqueur
- 2½ oz. (75 ml) Soda Water

Muddle the lychee, limes, mint leaves, and simple syrup in a glass. Add ice and other ingredients. Garnish with mint sprigs, lime slices, and lychee.

The Banana Leaf Restaurant in Vancouver, Canada has one of the best lychee mojitos ever. This recipe was inspired by their creation.

STRAWBERRY MOJITO

- 3 Strawberries
- 10 Mint Leaves
- 2 Lime Wedges
- 1½ oz. (45 ml) Simple Syrup
- 1½ oz. (45 ml) White Rum
- 2½ oz. (75 ml) Soda Water

Muddle the strawberries, limes, mint leaves, and simple syrup in a glass. Add ice and other ingredients. Garnish with mint sprigs, lime slices, and strawberry.

Margaritas

At every house party, there's always someone claiming to be an expert at making margaritas. He or she then promptly grabs a bottle of magarita mix and immediately my soul sinks. Experts don't use magarita mix! That's like someone claiming to be an expert mountain climber but always taking an escalator to the top. These simple recipes will have your friends refering to you as, "The Margarita Expert."

You can muddle or blend these margaritas. Muddling is easier than blending, especially at parties, where ice is always the first thing to run out. When you muddle, you use less ice and there's less to clean. Also, it tastes just as good, if not better, than blending. Now you don't have to wait in line behind the drunk dude that's hogging the blender. He's at every party. Who keeps inviting him?

Note * With these margaritas, you can rim your glass with salt or sugar, depending on your peference. And you can use your choice of lime juice or sour mix as the main mixer. In the photos, I used lime juice. However, sour mix is sweeter and more commonly used.

Margaritas

PINK MARGARITA

- 1 oz. (30 ml) Tequila
- ½ oz. (15 ml) Triple Sec
- ½ oz. (15 ml) Lime Juice
- 3 oz. (90 ml) Pink Lemonade

Build over ice in a glass rimmed with salt or sugar. Drink can also be served blended. Garnish with lime slices.

Only when tequila is produced in Mexico can it legally be called tequila, because Mexico owns all rights to the word "tequila." If you were to go in your backyard and make a bottle of booze using the same ingredients and production process as a Mexican tequila company, you still couldn't call in tequila unless you lived in Mexico.

BABY BLUE MARGARITA

- 1 oz. (30 ml) Silver Tequila
- ½ oz. (15 ml) Blue Curacao
- ¾ oz. (22 ml) Simple Syrup
- 3 oz. (90 ml) Sour Mix or Lime Juice

Pour everything except blue curacao over ice in a glass rimmed with salt or sugar. Float the blue curacao on top. Garnish with a lime.

This drink is so pretty you will not want to drink it. I almost came to tears as I drank mine. It felt like I was destroying a Picasso.

Tipsy Bartender: "I'm Having a Girl Over"

MELON MARGARITA

- ½ cup Honeydew Melon
- 1 oz. (30 ml) Tequila
- ½ oz. (15 ml) Triple Sec
- 1 oz. (30 ml) Simple Syrup
- 3 oz. (90 ml) Sour Mix or Lime Juice

Muddle honeydew and simple syrup in a glass rimmed with salt or sugar. Add ice and other ingredients. Drink can also be served blended. Garnish with lime slices and honeydew slice.

FRESH STRAWBERRY MARGARITA

- 4 Strawberries
- 1 oz. (30 ml) Tequila
- ½ oz. (15 ml) Triple Sec
- 1 oz. (30 ml) Simple Syrup
- 3 oz. (90 ml) Sour Mix or Lime Juice

Muddle strawberries and simple syrup in a glass rimmed with salt or sugar. Add ice and other ingredients. Drink can also be served blended. Garnish with lime slices and strawberries.

I live in LA, which means I'm usually on a diet. I know what you're thinking, "Dude, you diet?" Everybody in LA is on a diet! It's the law! But these fruit margaritas make me feel like I'm eating healthy. Two of these, and I've had my fruit salad for the day.

Margaritas

PEACH MARGARITA

- 1 Peach
- 1 oz. (30 ml) Tequila
- ½ oz. (15 ml) Peach Schnapps
- 1 oz. (30 ml) Simple Syrup
- 3 oz. (90 ml) Sour Mix or Lime Juice

Muddle peach and simple syrup in a glass rimmed with salt or sugar. Add ice and other ingredients. Drink can also be served blended. Garnish with lime and peach.

WATERMELON MARGARITA

- ½ cup Watermelon
- 1 oz. (30 ml) Tequila
- ½ oz. (15 ml) Triple Sec
- 1 oz. (30 ml) Simple Syrup
- 3 oz. (90 ml) Sour Mix or Lime Juice

Muddle watermelon and simple syrup in a glass rimmed with salt or sugar. Add ice and other ingredients. Drink can also be served blended. Garnish with lime and watermelon.

Tipsy Bartender: "I'm Having a Girl Over"

MANGO MARGARITA

- ½ cup Mango
- 1 oz. (30 ml) Tequila
- ½ oz. (15 ml) Triple Sec
- 1 oz. (30 ml) Simple Syrup
- 3 oz. (90 ml) Sour Mix or Lime Juice

Muddle mango and simple syrup in a glass rimmed with salt or sugar. Add ice and other ingredients. Drink can also be served blended. Garnish with lime slices and mango.

When you rim a glass with salt, use sea salt or kosher salt, not table salt. Sea salt and kosher salt have large grains. Table salt, on the other hand, has very fine grains. Therefore, a teaspoon of table salt contains more sodium than a teaspoon of kosher salt or sea salt. A drink rimmed with table salt would taste extremely salty.

PASSION FRUIT MARGARITA

- 1 oz. (30 ml) Tequila
- ½ oz. (15 ml) Triple Sec
- ½ oz. (15 ml) Lime Juice
- 3 oz. (90 ml) Passion Fruit Juice or Passion Fruit Nectar

Build over ice in a glass rimmed with salt or sugar. Drink can also be served blended. Garnish with lime.

Frozen Drinks and Ice Cream

    I love frozen cocktails. Sometime when I'm having a float, people give me that look of, "Ice cream floats are for kids." I let them know, "I'm a man! I pay taxes! And this is loaded with booze!" They respect you then, and usually ask you to make them one, too.

MUDSLIDE FLOAT

- ½ oz. (15 ml) Vodka
- ½ oz. (15 ml) Irish Cream
- ½ oz. (15 ml) Coffee Liqueur
- ½ oz. (15 ml) Butterscotch Schnapps
- 4 scoops of Vanilla Ice Cream

Pour liquor into a glass. Top with ice cream. Garnish with chocolate syrup and a cherry.

The mudslide is usually served as a mixed drink or as a blended drink. I like mine as an ice cream float.

Tipsy Bartender: "I'm Having a Girl Over"

SPIKED VANILLA ROOT BEER FLOAT

- 1½ oz. (45 ml) Vanilla Vodka
- 3 oz. (90 ml) Root Beer
- 3 scoops Vanilla Ice Cream

Pour vodka and root beer into a glass. Top with ice cream. Add cherry.

Spiked floats are amazing because the mixture of soda and ice cream makes the taste of alcohol very subtle.

SPIKED ORANGE CREAMSICLE FLOAT

- 1½ oz. (45 ml) Orange Vodka
- 3 oz. (90 ml) Orange Soda
- 3 scoops Vanilla Ice Cream

Pour vodka and orange soda into a glass. Top with ice cream. Add cherry.

Frozen Drinks and Ice Cream

SPIKED PINEAPPLE FLOAT

- 1½ oz. (45 ml) Rum
- 3 oz. (90 ml) Pineapple Juice
- 3 scoops Pineapple Coconut Ice Cream

Pour rum and pineapple juice into a glass. Top with ice cream. Garnish with a cherry and coconut sprinkles.

This one is rum based, tropical, and super delicious. I took a sip and felt like Captain Jack Sparrow sailing the seven seas.

STRAWBERRY DAIQUIRI

- 1 cup Frozen Strawberries
- 1½ oz. (45 ml) White Rum
- 1½ oz. (45 ml) Simple Syrup
- ½ oz. Grenadine

Add ice and blend all the ingredients except the rum. Pour the rum into a glass and add the blended ingredients on top. Garnish with a strawberry.

Usually when people blend daiquiris, they blend everything together at once. In the Bahamas, they always add the rum separately, and it makes a huge difference. This is my favorite drink.

Tipsy Bartender: "I'm Having a Girl Over"

PIÑA COLADA

- 1½ oz. (45 ml) White Rum
- 1½ oz. (45 ml) Cream of Coconut
- 3 oz. (90 ml) Pineapple Juice
- 1 oz. (30 ml) Pineapple Chunks

Blend all the ingredients except the rum with ice. Pour the rum into a glass and add the blended ingredients on top. Garnish with pineapple and a cherry.

The Piña Colada was created in Puerto Rico and is their national drink. If you have difficulty finding fresh pineapple, use canned pineapple slices. Your drink will be equally as awesome.

STRAWBERRY SHAKE

- 1½ oz. (45 ml) Vodka
- ½ oz. (15 ml) Strawberry Syrup
- ¾ pint Vanilla Ice Cream

Blend all ingredients, including the strawberry syrup. Serve in a glass garnished with strawberry syrup. Top with whipped cream and a cherry.

Frozen Drinks and Ice Cream

BANANA FOSTER COCKTAIL

- 1 Banana
- 1 oz. (30 ml) Spiced Rum
- 1 oz. (30 ml) Crème de Banana
- 1½ oz. (45 ml) Heavy Whipping Cream
- ½ oz. (15 ml) Carmel Syrup

Blend all the ingredients, including the caramel syrup, with ice. Serve in glass lined with caramel syrup. Top with whipped cream, nutmeg, and banana slices.

Every girl I've ever made this drink for loves it. I mean LOVES IT!

FUNFETTI CAKE BATTER MILKSHAKE

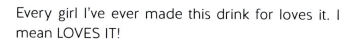

- 1½ oz. (45 ml) Cake Vodka
- 4 oz. (120 ml) Funfetti Cake Mix
- ¾ pint Vanilla Ice Cream

Blend all ingredients. Serve in glass rimmed with sprinkles. Use corn syrup to get sprinkles to hold. Add cherry.

Ladies and gentlemen, this drink is a winner. It is unparalleled greatest! This is what the gods drink. Zeus is sitting back in a recliner right now sipping on one of these. It's that good!

Cocktails

Okay people, it's happy hour, and time for us to enjoy some cocktails. I remember going to happy hour when I worked an office job. The boss would always want to join us. Happy hour is the time you let your hair down after a hard day's work. The last person you want sitting at your table is the boss! To all the bosses of the world, please be considerate and just go home. Your employees are about to get wild, and they don't want you judging them.

PEACHES AND BERRIES

- 2 Strawberries
- 1 oz. (30 ml) Vodka
- ½ oz. (15 ml) Peach Schnapps
- ½ oz. (15 ml) Simple Syrup
- Splash of Sour Mix
- 3 oz. (90 ml) Lemon-Lime Soda

Muddle strawberries and simple syrup in a glass. Add ice and other ingredients. Garnish with a strawberry, strawberry slices, and lime slices.

This is another one of those drinks that is just plain gorgeous. I would kill to date a girl as sexy as this drink. Although, you have to make it with fresh fruits, withered strawberries and wrinkled limes kill the sex appeal.

Cocktails

BLUE LAGOON

- 1 oz. (30 ml) Orange Vodka
- ½ oz. (15 ml) Blue Curacao
- 4 oz. (120 ml) Lemonade

Pour orange vodka and lemonade in a glass over ice. Float the blue curacao on top. Garnish with a lemon slice and a cherry.

Some say this drink is based on the 80's Brooke Shield's movie *Blue Lagoon*. My parents would always refer to that movie as being porn. I finally watched it as an adult, and by today's standards, that's like a Disney flick with a little bit of boobs. Mom and Dad, you guys need to spend more time on the Internet.

SNICKER LICKER

- 1 oz. (30 ml) Irish Cream
- 1 oz. (30 ml) Crème de Cacao
- ½ oz. (15 ml) Hazelnut Liqueur
- 2 oz. (60 ml) Milk

Garnish the inside of a glass with caramel and chocolate syrup. Add ice and pour in the ingredients. Add a cherry.

One night while I was bartending, my girlfriend at the time stopped in and I made her this drink. Every girl in the bar suddenly wanted one, to the point where we ran out of caramel syrup. One of the girls ran down the street to the supermarket and bought caramel syrup, just so we could keep making this drink. It's that good.

Tipsy Bartender: "I'm Having a Girl Over"

STRAWBERRY MOSCATO LEMONADE

- 2 Strawberries
- 1 oz. (30 ml) Lemonade
- 4 oz. (120 ml) Moscato

Muddle strawberries in a glass. Add lemonade and moscato. Garnish with strawberry and lemon slices.

CANDY SEX ON THE BEACH

- 1 oz. (30 ml) Vodka
- ½ oz. (15 ml) Peach Schnapps
- 1½ oz. (45 ml) Orange Juice
- 1½ oz. (45 ml) Cranberry Juice
- Splash of Pineapple Juice

Build over ice. Serve in sugar-rimmed glass. Garnish with a cherry and an orange slice.

The sex on the beach is everything: a yummy cocktail with a dirty name that is sure to take any conversation into the inappropriate fun zone. I like to add a sugar rim and a splash of pineapple to mine.

Cocktails

MALIBU PINEAPPLE SPLASH

- 1½ oz. (45 ml) Malibu Coconut Rum
- 3 oz. (90 ml) Pineapple Juice
- Splash of Cranberry Juice

Build ingredients over ice. Garnish with a cherry.

The Malibu Pineapple is one of those drinks all bartenders keep in their back pocket for that girl who's new to drinking and is looking for something not too strong with the right amount of sweetness. I add just a splash of cranberry to mine to even everything out.

COCONUT WOO WOO

- 1 oz. (30 ml) Coconut Rum
- ½ oz. (15 ml) Peach Schnapps
- 3 oz. (90 ml) Cranberry Juice

Build over ice. Garnish with a cherry.

Tipsy Bartender: "I'm Having a Girl Over"

SOUTHERN BELLE

- 1 oz. (30 ml) Bourbon
- ½ oz. (15 ml) Triple Sec
- 2 oz. (60 ml) Orange Juice
- 2 oz. (60 ml) Pineapple Juice
- Splash of Grenadine

Pour liquor and juices into an ice-filled glass. Float grenadine on top. Add cherry.

I love the name of this drink. When you think of Southern belles, you think of innocence, manners, and grace. That's not what you think of when you think of bourbon. This Southern belle is a rebel.

MIDORI SOUR

- 1½ oz. (45 ml) Midori
- 2 oz. (60 ml) Sour Mix
- 1 oz. (30 ml) Lemon-Lime Soda

Build over ice. Garnish with a lemon slice and a cherry.

Another popular drink with the ladies. I like to add lemon-lime soda to mine. Kim Kardashian was the spokesperson for Midori for several years. It was a strange marriage because in several interviews she said that she didn't drink. You're selling it, but you don't use it? Anyway, everyone should have Midori in their home bar; it's a great melon liqueur.

Cocktails

PINK LEMONADE

- 1 oz. (30 ml) Lemon Vodka
- ½ oz. (15 ml) Raspberry Liqueur
- 4 oz. (120 ml) Lemonade

Pour lemon vodka and lemonade over ice in a sugar-rimmed glass. Float raspberry liqueur on top. Garnish with a lemon slice and cherry.

DIRTY SHIRLEY

- 1 ½ oz. (45 ml) Raspberry Vodka
- 4 oz. (120 ml) Lemon-Lime Soda
- ½ oz. (15 ml) Grenadine

Pour raspberry vodka and lemon-lime soda in glass of ice. Float grenadine on top. Garnish with a cherry.

Tipsy Bartender: "I'm Having a Girl Over"

TOBLERONE

- 1 oz. (30 ml) Irish Cream
- 1 oz. (30 ml) Coffee Liqueur
- ½ oz. (15 ml) Hazelnut Liqueur
- 2 oz. (60 ml) Cream
- 1 Tbsp. Honey

Build ingredients over ice. Garnish with a cherry.

PEACH WINE COOLER

- 4 oz. (120 ml) White Wine
- ½ oz. (15 ml) Peach Schnapps
- ½ oz. (15 ml) Syrup from canned peaches

Build in a glass. Garnish with a canned peach half. The peach half is super tasty after being in your drink, so be sure and eat it!

Cocktails

HONEYDEW MIMOSA

- 1½ oz. Honeydew Chunks
- ½ oz. (15 ml) Simple Syrup
- 4 oz. (120 ml) Champagne

Muddle honeydew and simple syrup in a glass. Add champagne. Garnish with honeydew slice.

CITRONELLA COOLER

- 1½ oz. (45 ml) Lemon Vodka
- ½ oz. (15 ml) Lime Juice
- 2 oz. (60 ml) Lemonade
- 1 oz. (30 ml) Cranberry Juice

Pour everything except the cranberry juice in a glass with ice. Float cranberry juice on top. Garnish with lime slice and cherry.

I introduced a female bartender to this drink. She loved it so much that it became her go-to drink for her female customers.

Tipsy Bartender: "I'm Having a Girl Over"

CROCODILE COOLER

- ¾ oz. (22 ml) Melon Liqueur
- ¾ oz. (22 ml) Lemon Vodka
- ½ oz. (15 ml) Triple Sec
- 2 oz. (60 ml) Sour Mix
- Fill with Lemon-Lime Soda

Build ingredients over ice. Garnish with lime slice and cherry.

MELON COOLER

- 1 oz. (30 ml) Melon Liqueur
- ½ oz. (15 ml) Peach Schnapps
- ½ oz. (15 ml) Raspberry Liqueur
- 4 oz. (120 ml) Pineapple Juice

Pour melon liqueur, peach schnapps, and pineapple juice in a glass with ice. Float raspberry liqueur on top. Add cherry.

Cocktails

COCO DE MAYO

- 1½ oz. (45 ml) Tequila
- ½ oz. (15 ml) Lemon Juice
- 1 oz. (30 ml) Cream of Coconut
- 3 oz. (90 ml) Pineapple Juice

Shake ingredients with ice until cream of coconut dissolves. Strain over ice in a glass rimmed with toasted coconut. Garnish with pineapple slice and cherry.

Most people think Cinco de Mayo is Mexico's Independence Day. It's actually the day the Mexican army defeated French forces in the Battle of Puebla; May 5th, 1862. But the roots of Cinco de Mayo aren't important; what's important is that it gives us a good excuse to drink!

On Cinco de Mayo, you definitely want to have Coco de Mayo. This drink is spectacular with its toasted coconut rim.

TEQUILA SUNRISE

- 1½ oz. (45 ml) Tequila
- 3 oz. (90 ml) Orange Juice
- Splash of Grenadine on Top

Pour tequila and orange juice into a glass of ice. Float grenadine on top. Garnish with lime slice and a cherry.

Tipsy Bartender: "I'm Having a Girl Over"

ALAMO SPLASH

- 1½ oz. (45 ml) Tequila
- 2 oz. (60 ml) Orange Juice
- 1 oz. (30 ml) Pineapple Juice
- ½ oz. (15 ml) Lemon-Lime Soda

Build over ice. Garnish with orange slice and a cherry.

LA BOMBA

- 1 oz. (30 ml) Gold Tequila
- ½ oz. (15 ml) Triple Sec
- 1½ oz. (45 ml) Pineapple Juice
- 1½ oz. (45 ml) Cranberry Juice
- Splash of Grenadine

Pour liquor and juices in a glass of ice. Float grenadine on top. Garnish with a lime slice and cherry.

La Bomba is a great drink, although most people confuse in with the song "La Bamba." Maybe at some point it was called La Bamba and some artsy dude, in an attempt to be edgy, spelled it "La Bomba." Call it what you want, it's a great drink.

Cocktails

SHANDY

- ½ pint Beer (Hefeweizens or light beers work best)
- ½ pint Lemonade or Lemon-Lime Soda

Half fill a pint glass with beer. Top with your choice of lemonade or lemon-lime soda. Garnish with a lemon slice.

Shandies are best when you use hefeweizens or lagers. Have you ever heard of a Guinness shandy? The mere thought of that seems repulsive, but rumor has it that the New Zealand rugby team mistakenly ordered Guinness shandies and everybody loved them!

HENNY COLADA

- 1½ oz. (45 ml) Hennessy
- 1½ oz. (45 ml) Cream of Coconut
- 4 oz. (120 ml) Pineapple Juice

Shake ingredients with ice until cream of coconut dissolves. Strain into an ice-filled glass garnished inside with caramel syrup.

You wouldn't expect to see Hennessy in a book like this, but the Henny Colada is pure gold. I made it for one of the sweetest, most innocent girls ever. She liked it so much she had one sip and chugged the rest.

Tipsy Bartender: "I'm Having a Girl Over"

MALIBU PRINCESS

- 1 oz. (30 ml) Malibu Coconut
- 1 oz. (30 ml) Melon Liqueur
- 4 oz. (120 ml) Pineapple Juice

Build over ice. Top with whipped cream. Add cherry.

AMARETTO SUNRISE

- 1½ oz. (45 ml) Amaretto
- 3 oz. (90 ml) Orange Juice
- Splash of Grenadine

Pour amaretto and orange juice into a glass of ice. Float grenadine on top. Garnish with orange slice and cherry.

LOVE CAKES

- 1½ oz. (45 ml) Cake Vodka
- 4 oz. (120 ml) Root Beer

Build over ice. Garnish with a cherry.

Cocktails

SWEET BANANA DREAM

- 1½ oz. (45 ml) Crème de Banana
- 4 oz. (120 ml) Root Beer

Build over ice. Add cherry.

GIN FUZZY LOGIC

- ¾ oz. (22 ml) Gin
- ¾ oz. (22 ml) Peach Schnapps
- 4 oz. (120 ml) Orange Juice

Build over ice. Add orange slice and a cherry.

BERMUDA TRIANGLE

- 1 oz. (30 ml) Spiced Rum
- ½ oz. (15 ml) Peach Schnapps
- 3 oz. (90 ml) Orange Juice

Build over ice. Add orange slice and cherry.

BUTTER CREAM PI

- 1 oz. (30 ml) Vanilla Vodka
- ½ oz. (15 ml) Butterscotch Schnapps
- 4 oz. (120 ml) Cream Soda

Build over ice. Add cherry.

When you think of shots, you think of pain, punishment, something you have to get psyched to do, and something you don't want to do when you have to work the next day. When guys do shots, we huddle together for the requiste prep talk: "We can do this! But we have to do it together! No one gets left behind!" You break huddle and it's a tense moment, because you know someone is not going to make it; you just hope that person is not you. As you hold your glass, sweat drips from your brow. Then someone shouts, "Bottoms up!" You all toast, throw your heads back, and pour it down the drain. In a single swallow, you manage to get it down. Your throat burns, your chest is on fire, your eyes water, and your nose is running. What the hell was that, gasoline?! You look over at Bill. He's coughing and convulsing. He may not make it. You rush over to him...and you laugh! That's how guys do shots!

None of the shots in this book require you to get psyched first. There are no burning chests, runny noses, or watery eyes associated with any of these shots. Everything here will go down smoothly. Bill would love this section.

Shots

CHOCOLATE-COVERED CHERRY

- ½ oz. (15 ml) Coffee liqueur
- ½ oz. (15 ml) Amaretto
- ½ oz. (15 ml) Chocolate liqueur
- Splash of Grenadine

Shake the ingredients with ice and strain into a shot glass garnished inside with chocolate syrup. Add strawberry coated in chocolate syrup on top.

It's a stunningly beautiful shot that tastes amazing.

PEDRO'S MELON BALL

- ½ oz. (15 ml) Vodka
- ½ oz. (15 ml) Melon Liqueur
- ½ oz. (15 ml) Peach Schnapps
- 1 oz. (30 ml) Pineapple Juice
- Splash Blue Curacao

Shake all the ingredients except the blue curacao with ice and strain into a shot glass. Float the blue curacao on top.

Pedro and I bartended together for a couple years. This is a great-tasting drink, but what really draws people in is the crazy colors. It's fun to make it and watch the colors change.

Tipsy Bartender: "I'm Having a Girl Over"

ALLIGATOR TAIL

- ½ oz. (15 ml) Grenadine
- ½ oz. (15 ml) Melon Liqueur
- ½ oz. (15 ml) Jägermeister

In order, layer grenadine, melon liqueur, and Jägermeister on top of one another using a spoon. Put the shot in the freezer for a minute to get cold before you shoot it. It'll taste better that way.

Layered drinks are spectacularly beautiful, but they often taste like grandpa's sweaty socks. That's because, firstly, bartenders focus more on the color combination than on the taste. Secondly, layered drinks are more often than not served at room temperature. Shots, in my opinion, go down a whole lot smoother if they're chilled. Slip this drink into the freezer for few minutes to get it cold and you'll have a scrumptious shot!

BLUE KAMIKAZE

- ½ oz. (15 ml) Vodka
- ½ oz. (15 ml) Simple Syrup
- ½ oz. (15 ml) Blue Curacao
- 1 oz. (30 ml) Lime Juice

Shake the ingredients with ice and strain into a shot glass. Add lime slice.

Shots

GEORGIA PEACH

- 1 oz. (30 ml) Peach Schnapps
- ½ oz. (15 ml) Southern Comfort
- 1 oz. (30 ml) Orange Juice
- Splash Grenadine

Shake all ingredients except the grenadine with ice and strain into a shot glass rimmed with sugar. Float grenadine on top. Add peach slice.

This is a fun, super-easy shot. Some girls from Georgia gave me this recipe. I added the sugar rim and the peach to make it even sexier.

WHITE GUMMY BEAR

- ½ oz. (15 ml) Raspberry Vodka
- ½ oz. (15 ml) Peach Schnapps
- ½ oz. (15 ml) Pineapple Juice
- 1 oz. (30 ml) Lemon-Lime Soda

Stir the ingredients with ice and strain into a shot glass. Add gummy bear.

The gummy bear garnish really sells this shot. When you see it, you immediately have to try it. How can you say no to a gummy bear sitting on your glass smiling at you? You have to play with it!

Tipsy Bartender: "I'm Having a Girl Over"

GREEN GUMMY BEAR

- ½ oz. (15 ml) Orange Vodka
- 1 oz. (30 ml) Melon Liqueur
- 1 oz. (30 ml) Lemon-Lime Soda

Stir the ingredients with ice and strain into a shot glass. Add gummy bears.

BLUE BALLS

- ½ oz. (15 ml) Coconut Rum
- ½ oz. (15 ml) Blue Curacao
- ½ oz. (15 ml) Peach Schnapps
- Splash of Sour Mix
- Splash of Lemon-Lime Soda

Shake the ingredients with ice and strain into a shot glass.

I love shots with dirty names because they allow you to flirt with female customers. "You guys want one of my blue balls?" "Wait until you taste my blue balls." I said something to that effect one night to two girls, and they laughed and we had a good time. Turns out they were both secret shoppers who promptly reported me to management and I was almost fired.

Shots

TRAVIS'S CRACK WHORE

- 1 oz. (30 ml) Strawberry Vodka
- ½ oz. (15 ml) Triple Sec
- Splash Sour Mix
- Splash Fresh Lime Juice
- 1 oz. (30 ml) Cranberry Juice

Shake the ingredients with ice and strain into a shot glass. Add lime slice.

I bartended every week with Travis, and this was his go-to shot. His customers, both men and women loved it. He could easily go through a bottle of strawberry vodka in one shift.

GREEN WATER MOCCASIN

- ½ oz. (15 ml) Whiskey
- ½ oz. (15 ml) Peach Schnapps
- ½ oz. (15 ml) Melon Liqueur
- Splash of Triple Sec
- 1 oz. (30 ml) Sour Mix

Shake the ingredients with ice and strain into a shot glass.

My friend Meghan from Florida created this drink. She jumped into my liquor collection and popped out with this colorful shot. I would also like to thank her for her help with this book.

Tipsy Bartender: "I'm Having a Girl Over"

HERSHEY SQUIRT SHOT

- 1 oz. (30 ml) Irish Cream
- ¾ oz. (22 ml) Butterscotch Schnapps
- 2 tbsp. Peanut Butter
- 1 tbsp. Chocolate Syrup

Shake the ingredients with ice and strain into a shot glass rimmed with peanut butter and garnished inside with chocolate syrup.

Peanut butter and alcohol seems like it would be a horrible combination. A marriage bound to end in divorce you may think, but it works so well. This is a really tasty shot. You won't be able to have just one. A girlfriend and I went through half a jar of peanut butter just doing Hershey Squirt shots.

PEANUT BUTTERY SHOT

- ½ oz. (15 ml) Vanilla Vodka
- ½ oz. (15 ml) Irish Cream
- ½ oz. (15 ml) Butterscotch
- 1 oz. (30 ml) Milk
- 1 tbsp. Peanut Butter

Shake the ingredients with ice and strain into a shot glass rimmed with peanut butter.

Shots

RASPBERRY LEMON DROP SHOT

- ½ oz. (15 ml) Vodka
- ½ oz. (15 ml) Raspberry Liqueur
- 1 oz. (30 ml) Lemon Juice
- ½ oz. (15 ml) Simple Syrup

Shake the ingredients with ice and strain into a shot glass rimmed with sugar. Add raspberry.

LIQUID MARIJUANA

- ½ oz. (15 ml) Spiced Rum
- ½ oz. (15 ml) Melon Liqueur
- ½ oz. (15 ml) Coconut Rum
- ½ oz. (15 ml) Blue Curacao
- ½ oz. (15 ml) Pineapple Juice
- Splash Sour Mix

Shake the ingredients with ice and strain into a shot glass.

Whenever I mention this shot to a newbie, the response is either, "No, I don't do drugs" or "Liquid pot! Where'd you get it?" There is no actual marijuana in this shot. It gets its name from the green color. This is another one of my favorites. It's tantalizing.

Tipsy Bartender: "I'm Having a Girl Over"

MANGO SHOOTER

- 1 oz. (30 ml) Vodka
- ½ oz. (15 ml) Simple Syrup
- Mango Slice

Shake the vodka and simple syrup with ice and strain into a shot glass. Place the mango on top of shot. After you take the shot, bite into the mango.

When you're thinking shots for the ladies, a shot of vodka isn't on the list. However, with simple syrup as a sweetener and biting into fresh delicious mango as the chaser, this shot works and works well!

FUZZY MONKEY

- ½ oz. (15 ml) Vodka
- ½ oz. (15 ml) Peach Schnapps
- ½ oz. (15 ml) Banana Liqueur
- 1 oz. (30 ml) Orange Juice

Shake the ingredients with ice and strain into a shot glass. Garnish with banana slices.

Shots

PEACHES & CREAM

- 1 oz. (30 ml) Peach Schnapps
- 1 oz. (30 ml) Heavy Cream
- Splash Grenadine

Shake all the ingredients except the grenadine with ice and strain into a shot glass. Float the grenadine on top.

BLOW JOB SHOT

- 1 oz. (30 ml) Irish Cream
- 1 oz. (30 ml) Amaretto

Shake the ingredients with ice and strain into a shot glass. Top with whipped cream.

To do this shot, lock your hands behind your back. Pick up the shot glass using only your mouth. Shoot it and put the glass back. NO HANDS! Now you understand the name.

This shot is dirty and it's fun. There were so many nights where we made huge batches of blow jobs and had the entire bar doing them. This shot will get any party started!

Tipsy Bartender: "I'm Having a Girl Over"

ORGASM SHOT

- ½ oz. (15 ml) Irish Cream
- ½ oz. (15 ml) Amaretto
- ½ oz. (15 ml) Coffee Liqueur

Shake the ingredients with ice and strain into a shot glass.

It's simple, smooth, and fun. And we haven't even gotten to its risqué name yet.

SCOOBY SNACK

- ½ oz. (15 ml) Coconut Rum
- ½ oz. (15 ml) Crème de Bananas
- ½ oz. (15 ml) Melon Liqueur
- ½ oz. (15 ml) Pineapple Juice
- 1 oz. (30 ml) Whipped Cream

Shake all the ingredients, including the whipped cream, with ice and strain into a shot glass. Top with whipped cream.

Scooby Snacks are another hugely popular shot that everyone loves, both guys and girls. I've never made just one Scooby Snack for a customer. It was always, "Gimme five Scooby Snacks." "Bartender, we need eight of them this time." It's a really good shot.

Shots

JUSTIN'S BIG OL' TITTIES

- ½ oz. (15 ml) Spiced Rum
- ½ oz. (15 ml) Coconut Rum
- ½ oz. (15 ml) Peach Schnapps
- 1 oz. (30 ml) Pineapple Juice
- Splash of Lemon-Lime Soda

Shake the ingredients with ice and strain into a shot glass.

I bartended with Justin many nights. This was his go-to shot for the ladies. The night he created it, he asked a girl what he should call it and she said, "Big Ol' Titties." We all loved the name and went with it.

BUTTERY NIPPLE

- 1 oz. (30 ml) Irish Cream
- 1 oz. (30 ml) Butterscotch Schnapps

Shake the ingredients with ice and strain into a shot glass.

If you love creamy drinks, then you'll definitely enjoy buttery nipples. We had a regular named Jay and whenever he bought a girl a shot, it was always this one.

Tipsy Bartender: "I'm Having a Girl Over"

BLONDE-HEADED SLUT

- ½ oz. (15 ml) Jägermeister
- ½ oz. (15 ml) Peach Schnapps
- 1 oz. (30 ml) Pineapple Juice

Shake the ingredients with ice and strain into a shot glass.

Don't let the Jägermeister scare you away. This is a sweet shot that goes down super easy. I like this version more than its more popular sister, The Redheaded Slut, where cranberry juice is used instead of pineapple juice.

RASPBERRY TROUBLE

- ½ oz. (15 ml) Peach Schnapps
- ½ oz. (15 ml) Raspberry Liqueur
- 1 oz. (30 ml) Lemon-Lime Soda

Stir the ingredients with ice and strain into a shot glass.

HONEYSUCKLE SHOT

- 1 oz. (30 ml) Rum
- ½ oz. (15 ml) Lime Juice
- ½ oz. (15 ml) Honey

Shake the ingredients with ice and strain into a shot glass.

Bombs

How can you make a shot something more? By turning it into an event: a Bomb! Bombs are done by dropping a shot glass filled with booze into a pint glass that's half filled with another liquid and then chugging both mixtures all at once. It's always a race to see who can finish first.

Bombs often contain more alcohol than a regular shot. The Irish Car Bomb is a mix of three different alcohols: Guinness Stout, Jameson Irish Whiskey, and Baileys Irish Cream. But the Bombs listed in this section are not going to knock you off your feet. They are all easily doable and super tasty.

ITALIAN BOMB

- 1 oz. (30 ml) Amaretto
- ¼ pint Energy Drink
- ¼ pint Orange Juice
- Splash of Grenadine

Shake the amaretto with ice and strain into a shot glass. In a pint glass, pour the energy drink, orange juice, and splash of grenadine.

Tipsy Bartender: "I'm Having a Girl Over"

VEGAS BOMB

- ¼ oz. (7 ml) Whiskey
- ¼ oz. (7 ml) Coconut Rum
- ¼ oz. (7 ml) Peach Schnapps
- ¼ oz. (7 ml) Cranberry
- ½ pint of Energy Drink

Shake all the ingredients except the energy drink with ice and strain into a shot glass. In a pint glass, pour the energy drink.

CACTUS COOLER BOMB

- ½ oz. (15 ml) Orange Vodka
- ½ oz. (15 ml) Peach Schnapps
- ½ pint of Energy Drink
- Splash Orange Juice

Shake the vodka and peach schnapps with ice and strain into a shot glass. Into a pint glass, pour the Red Bull and splash of orange juice.

Bombs

JÄGER MONSTER BOMB

- 1 oz. (30 ml) Jägermeister
- ½ pint of Orange Juice
- Splash of Grenadine

Pour cold Jägermeister into a shot glass. In a pint glass, pour the orange juice and a splash of grenadine.

COCONUT BOMB

- 1 oz. (30 ml) Coconut Rum
- ½ pint Energy Drink
- Splash Pineapple Juice

Shake the coconut rum with ice and strain into a shot glass. In a pint glass, pour the energy drink and splash of pineapple juice.

Special Note to the Reader

I love to party hard. We've all had our share of all-nighters, especially the ones where you know you have work in the morning. Those are real killers! Just remember to always drink responsibly. We drink for a nice buzz, to relax, to take the edge off, never to get wasted. Whatever you do, always take a taxi or use a designated driver. **Never drink and drive!** Now go mix some drinks!

AND THERE YOU HAVE IT!

Index

Alamo Splash – 42
Alligator Tail – 48
Amaretto Sunrise – 44
Appletini – 7
Baby Blue Margarita 23
Banana Foster – 31
Bellini Martini – 18
Bermuda Triangle – 45
Blonde-Headed Slut – 58
Blow Job Shot – 55
Blue Balls – 50
Blue Kamikaze – 48
Blue Lagoon – 33
Brandy Alexander – 15
Butter Cream Pie – 45
Buttery Nipple 57
Cactus Cooler Bomb – 60
Cake Batter Martini – 4
Candy Sex on the Beach – 34
Caramel Appletini – 8
Chocolate Martini – 9
Chocolate-Covered Cherry – 47
Citronella Cooler – 39

Coco de Mayo – 41
Coconut Bomb – 61
Coconut Martini – 6
Coconut Woo Woo – 35
Cosmopolitan – 16
Cotton Candy Martini – 12
Cran-Appletini – 7
Crocodile Cooler – 40
Dirty Shirley – 37
French Martini – 18
Fresh Strawberry Margarita – 24
Funfetti Cake Batter Milkshake – 31
Fuzzy Monkey – 54
Georgia Peach – 49
German Chocolate Cake Martini – 5
Gin Fuzzy Logic – 45
Glamour Girl Martini – 12
Green Gummy Bear – 50
Green Water Moccasin – 51
Henny Colada – 43
Hershey Squirt Shot – 52
Honeydew Mimosa – 39
Honeysuckle Shot – 58

Tipsy Bartender: "I'm Having a Girl Over"

Ice Cream Martini – 8
Italian Bomb – 59
Jager Monster Bomb – 61
Justin's Big Ol'Titties – 57
Key Lime Pie – 13
Kiw-Tini – 15
La Bomba – 42
Lemon Drop Martini – 14
Lemon Merinigue Martini – 11
Liquid Marijuana – 53
Love Cakes – 44
Lychee Martini – 17
Lychee Mojito – 21
Malibu Pineapple Splash – 35
Malibu Princess – 44
Mango Margarita – 26
Mango Mojito – 20
Mango Shooter – 54
Melon Cooler – 40
Melon Margarita – 24
Mexi-Tini – 13
Midori Sour – 36
Mojito – 20
Mudslide Float – 27
Orange Creamsicle Martini – 11
Orgasm shot – 56
Passion Fruit Margarita – 26
Peach Margarita – 25
Peach Wine Cooler – 38
Peaches & Cream – 55
Peaches and Berries – 32
Peanut Buttery Shot – 52
Peartini – 16
Pedro's Melon Ball – 47
Piña Colada – 30

Pink Lemonade – 37
Pink Margarita – 23
Raspberry Lemon Drop Shot – 53
Raspberry Martini – 4
Raspberry Trouble – 58
Scooby Snack – 56
Shandy – 43
Simple Syrup –2
Snicker Licker – 33
Snickerdoodle – 14
Sour Mix –. 2
Southern Belle – 36
Spiked Orange Creamsicle Float – 28
Spiked Pineapple Float – 29
Spiked Vanilla Root Beer Float -28
Strawberry Daiquiri – 29
Strawberry Mojito 21
Strawberry Moscato Lemonade – 34
Strawberry Shake – 30
Sweet & Sour – 2
Sweet Banana Dream – 45
Tequila Sour Apple Martini – 17
Tequila Sunrise – 41
Tipsy Breakfast Martini – 5
Tiramisu Martini – 9
Toblerone – 38
Travis' Crack Whore – 51
Tropical Jade Martini – 6
Vegas Bomb – 60
Watermelon Margarita – 25
Watermelon Martini – 3
Whiskey Martini – 10
White Chocolate Martini – 10
White Gummy Bear – 49

Made in the USA
San Bernardino, CA
19 August 2016